SAVING ANIMALS

SAVING GREEN SEA TURTLES

by Martha London

T0015959

FOCUS
READERS.

NAVIGATOR

WWW.FOCUSREADERS.COM

Focus Readers is distributed by North Star Editions:
sales@northstareditions.com | 888-417-0195

Produced for Focus Readers by Red Line Editorial.

Content Consultant: Kate L. Mansfield, PhD, Associate Professor of Biology, University of Central Florida

Photographs ©: Shutterstock Images, cover, 1, 7, 9 (Cocos Island), 9 (Galapagos Island), 13, 15, 19, 21, 22–23; John Burns/NOAA, 4–5; Michael Patrick O'Neill/Science Source, 10–11; Jeff Rotman/Science Source, 16–17; Rob Griffith/AP Images, 25; Christoph Reichwein/picture-alliance/dpa/AP Images, 27; Ali Bayless/NMFS/PIFSC/NOAA, 29

Library of Congress Cataloging-in-Publication Data
Names: London, Martha, author.
Title: Saving green sea turtles / by Martha London.
Description: Lake Elmo, MN : Focus Readers, [2021] | Series: Saving animals | Includes index. | Audience: Grades 4-6
Identifiers: LCCN 2020004000 (print) | LCCN 2020004001 (ebook) | ISBN 9781644933862 (hardcover) | ISBN 9781644934623 (paperback) | ISBN 9781644936146 (pdf) | ISBN 9781644935385 (ebook)
Subjects: LCSH: Green turtle--Conservation--Juvenile literature.
Classification: LCC QL666.C536 L68 2021 (print) | LCC QL666.C536 (ebook) | DDC 597.92/8--dc23
LC record available at https://lccn.loc.gov/2020004000
LC ebook record available at https://lccn.loc.gov/2020004001

Printed in the United States of America
Mankato, MN
012021

ABOUT THE AUTHOR

Martha London writes books for young readers. When she isn't writing, you can find her hiking in the woods.

TABLE OF CONTENTS

CHAPTER 1

GRAZING ON GRASS

Green sea turtles make their homes in warm ocean waters around the world. Young green sea turtles live their first few years in the open ocean. But as they get older, green turtles tend to live near shore. Some adult green turtles live in **lagoons** and bays. Others live on **coral reefs**.

As adults, green sea turtles can weigh up to 700 pounds (320 kg).

Young green sea turtles eat small crabs and jellyfish. They also eat seagrass and algae. As they become older, they switch to only eating plants. The turtles' beaks have adapted to these foods. The beaks are sharp and have grooves. Green turtles also have a strong bite.

HUNDREDS OF EGGS

Green sea turtles typically lay eggs every two years. A female turtle can lay more than 100 eggs at one time. First, the green turtle lays its eggs on a beach. Then, it covers the eggs with sand. After that, the female turtle returns to the ocean. Two months later, the eggs hatch. Most of the babies are eaten by predators. Very few survive to become adults.

These features help green sea turtles chew seagrass. They chomp off the tops of grasses. However, green sea turtles do not rip the grasses out from their roots. In this way, the turtles help their **habitats** stay healthy.

GREEN SEA TURTLE RANGE

MILES OF MIGRATION

Some green sea turtles travel thousands of miles every year. Adults **migrate** from feeding areas to nesting grounds every two years. Nesting and feeding areas can be more than 1,300 miles (2,100 km) away from one another.

Scientists often track green sea turtles as they migrate. In 2014, a group of scientists tracked three green turtles. The turtles traveled from Cocos Island to the Galapagos Islands. These islands lie west of South America in the Pacific Ocean. The islands are protected areas. In protected areas, people are not allowed to harm plants or animals.

The green sea turtles were safe in their feeding and nesting areas. But the turtles were not safe

FROM COCOS TO GALAPAGOS

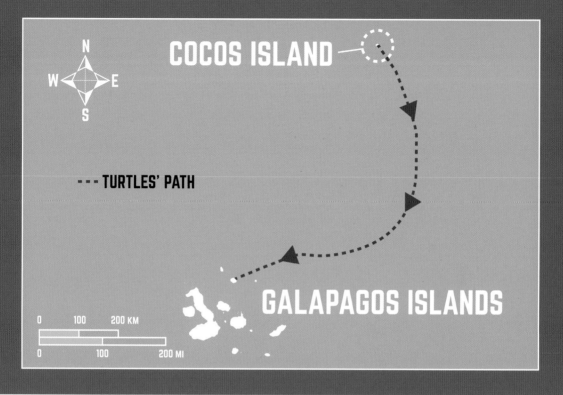

COCOS ISLAND

N
W — E
S

- - - TURTLES' PATH

GALAPAGOS ISLANDS

0   100   200 KM

0   100   200 MI

during their travel between those areas. Scientists had tracked sea turtles during that travel. They hoped their research and findings would lead to more migration paths being protected. By protecting those travel paths, green sea turtles would be safe for more of their lifespans.

CHAPTER 2

HEALTHY TURTLES, HEALTHY OCEANS

Green sea turtles help **ecosystems** in a variety of ways. One way is by eating algae. Certain kinds of algae grow on hard surfaces underwater. One common surface is coral. Coral are living animals. Some algae are good for the coral. But large amounts of algae choke the coral. In addition, algae grow on seagrass.

A green sea turtle eats algae off the coast of Florida.

Large amounts of algae can kill seagrass as well.

By eating algae, green turtles stop algae from growing too much. In this way, turtles help keep seagrass beds and coral reefs healthy. Helping these areas survive

SEAGRASS BEDS

Tens of millions of green sea turtles used to live in the Caribbean Sea. The area's seagrass beds were healthy. However, in the 1980s, scientists noticed that seagrass beds were dying. The seagrass was collecting fungi and algae. Slime molds were growing on the grass. Then scientists noticed that green sea turtle numbers were low. Fewer turtles were around to eat the old seagrass. As a result, infection had spread throughout the seagrass beds.

Green sea turtles have a favorite kind of seagrass. For this reason, it is often known as turtle grass.

is not just important for turtles. Seagrass beds provide homes and nesting areas for fish and other animals. Coral reefs provide homes to nearly 25 percent of all ocean life. When seagrass beds and reefs die, all of that sea life can suffer.

Humans also depend on green sea turtles, reefs, and seagrass. For example, the Miskito people of Nicaragua rely on green sea turtles. These people have fished green turtles for hundreds of years. The turtles are also important to Miskito culture.

In addition, many people eat other kinds of seafood from reefs and seagrass beds. These areas are home to fish, shrimp, and crabs. People in coastal towns often fish and harvest these animals. These activities provide jobs for workers in those communities. The seafood also provides food to people around the world.

Coral reefs support a huge variety of life. That's why they are sometimes called the rainforests of the sea.

When reefs and seagrass beds die, towns can lose important parts of their economies. It can be harder for some people to get seafood to eat. By keeping reefs and seagrass beds healthy, green sea turtles help animals, plants, and people around the world survive.

CHAPTER 3

IN DANGER

Green sea turtle populations have been falling for years. These turtles face several threats. For example, some fishers cast huge nets into the ocean. The nets catch seafood such as shrimp. But they also catch turtles by accident. Fishing hooks can also kill turtles by accident. These problems are called bycatch.

Between 1900 and 2018, the number of green sea turtles dropped by at least half.

Humans also destroy turtles' nesting areas. This happens because many people want to live near the ocean. They build homes along the shore. The buildings reduce the amount of beach turtles can use. These actions make it harder for green sea turtles to lay eggs.

People use green sea turtles for food as well. Some people harvest turtle eggs. Others kill green turtles for their meat. Green sea turtles are at risk, so these actions are illegal in certain countries. Even so, people do not always follow these laws.

People harm green sea turtles in less direct ways, too. Plastic is one major way.

A baby green sea turtle makes its way to the ocean after hatching on the beach.

Millions of tons of plastic enter the ocean each year. People use approximately one million plastic bags every minute. These bags are especially harmful to young green turtles. Floating plastic bags look like jellyfish. When turtles try to eat the bags, they choke.

Climate change is another major threat to green sea turtles. This crisis is causing sea levels to rise. Climate change is making strong storms more common, too.

Both of these changes will destroy green turtles' beach habitats.

In addition, a green turtle becomes male or female based on the temperature of the nest. Cooler temperatures usually result in male turtles. Warmer temperatures tend to result in female turtles. Climate change is increasing Earth's average temperatures. As a result, more female turtles are hatching. In the future, there may not be enough males to mate with all the females.

Finally, climate change is affecting Earth's oceans. Water temperatures are rising. The crisis is also increasing **ocean acidity**. These changes are killing large

When water temperature or acidity is too high, corals get rid of their colorful algae. The corals turn white.

parts of coral reefs. The reefs' algae are dying as well. With fewer reefs, many green turtles are losing their homes. With less algae, the turtles are losing a major food source. As climate change becomes more serious, these dangers will increase.

CHAPTER 4

PROTECTING GREEN SEA TURTLES

Green sea turtles need help to survive. For example, people can use less plastic. Addressing climate change is also one of the best ways to help. Countries need to change how they get energy. Countries mostly use fossil fuels for energy. These fuels include oil and gas. They power cars, electricity, and more.

As of 2020, coal power was the biggest cause of climate change.

However, burning these fuels releases carbon dioxide into the air. This kind of gas makes climate change worse.

To slow climate change, countries must use far fewer fossil fuels. They must switch to other energy sources, such as wind and solar energy. People can demand these changes from their governments. Slowing climate change can help coral reefs. And it can make sure enough male green sea turtles are born.

Scientists are studying green turtles. Some scientists catch turtles. They measure the turtles' shells. This tells scientists the turtles' ages. Scientists take blood samples, too. They test the

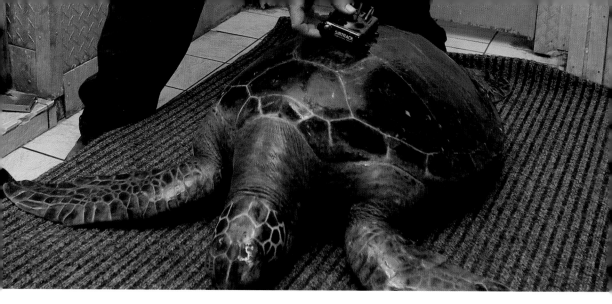

A scientist places a tracker on a rescued green sea turtle in Australia.

blood for diseases. This information tells scientists about the turtles' health.

Scientists also attach trackers to the shells of these turtles. Then they release the turtles. The trackers send signals to satellites in space. Scientists can see where the turtles travel. Tracking tells scientists where adult green turtles spend the most time eating and nesting.

These areas are important to protect. It's also important to protect the travel paths between feeding and nesting areas. Without nesting areas, turtles cannot reproduce.

Conservation groups are helping to protect green turtle habitats. Some groups are cleaning beaches where these turtles visit. They also are trying to limit the amount of building on these beaches.

However, the open ocean needs to be protected as well. That is why some conservation groups are working to protect the Cocos-Galapagos Swimway. This area stretches between Cocos Island and the Galapagos Islands. It also

A scientist helps protect a green sea turtle nest as babies hatch on a beach in Mexico.

stretches north of Cocos Island to Central America. Many green sea turtles use this area to migrate.

If the swimway was protected, less fishing would take place there. Then fewer green sea turtles would be killed.

Conservation groups are working with the governments of Costa Rica and Ecuador to protect this area.

In addition, some groups are working with fishers to limit bycatch. Fishing hooks can have many different shapes.

LIGHTING LAWS

Baby green sea turtles look for light shining off the ocean when they hatch. Moonlight often helps lead the turtles to the water. But light from buildings can confuse baby turtles. They head toward the buildings instead. As a result, many turtles get eaten by predators. Others become too tired. For this reason, some coastal cities allow fewer lights to shine during nesting season. In Florida, these efforts have helped save thousands of baby turtles.

Between 2002 and 2015, the number of green sea turtles around Hawaii and other US Pacific islands increased.

Some shapes are less likely to catch turtles. Also, fishers can use a different type of net. These nets have lights on them. The turtles can see the nets and avoid them.

Saving green sea turtles will take a great deal of effort. But many people are working hard to make sure green sea turtles will recover.

FOCUS ON
SAVING GREEN SEA TURTLES

Write your answers on a separate piece of paper.

1. Write a paragraph that explains the key ideas from Chapter 2.

2. Green sea turtles need beaches for nests. Do you think people should be allowed to build houses near green sea turtle nesting sites? Why or why not?

3. What kind of light helps baby green sea turtles reach the ocean from the beach?

    A. building light
    B. moonlight
    C. car light

4. Conservation groups are restoring nesting beaches. How will this action help green sea turtles?

    A. Baby green sea turtles will not be hurt by lights.
    B. Climate change will slow down.
    C. Green sea turtles will have enough space to make nests.

Answer key on page 32.

GLOSSARY

climate change
A human-caused global crisis involving long-term changes in Earth's temperature and weather patterns.

conservation
The careful protection of plants, animals, and natural resources so they are not lost or wasted.

coral reefs
Systems of animals that live in warm, shallow waters.

ecosystems
Communities of living things and how they interact with their surrounding environments.

habitats
The types of places where plants or animals normally grow or live.

lagoons
Shallow bodies of water that connect to seas or oceans.

migrate
To move from one region to another.

ocean acidity
A human-caused change in the chemical properties of ocean water that causes coral skeletons and animal shells to weaken.

TO LEARN MORE

BOOKS

Grunbaum, Mara. *Sea Turtles*. New York: Scholastic, 2018.

Machajewski, Sarah. *Saving the Endangered Green Sea Turtle*. New York: Rosen Educational Services, 2016.

Miller, Mirella S. *Sea Turtles Are Awesome*. Mankato, MN: 12-Story Library, 2018.

NOTE TO EDUCATORS

Visit **www.focusreaders.com** to find lesson plans, activities, links, and other resources related to this title.

INDEX

Answer Key: 1. Answers will vary; **2.** Answers will vary; **3.** B; **4.** C